# STORMALONG
## and the
# Giant
# Octopus

## Based on an American tall tale

Retold by Tom Davison

**NATIONAL GEOGRAPHIC**

L E A R N I N G

One morning, many years ago, a big wave carried a giant turtle onto a beach in the United States. The turtle had a giant human baby on its back. This was not a normal baby. This baby was bigger than three grown men!

The family that found the baby called him
Alfred B. Stormalong. But they called him Stormy.
They looked after him, and Stormy grew even bigger.
When he was a boy, he was bigger than a whale.
In fact, he had two whales for pets!

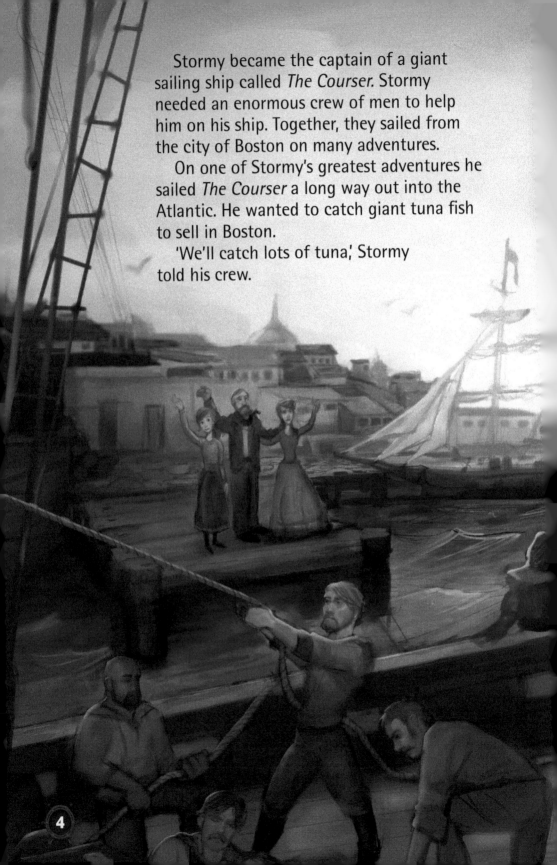

Stormy became the captain of a giant sailing ship called *The Courser*. Stormy needed an enormous crew of men to help him on his ship. Together, they sailed from the city of Boston on many adventures.

On one of Stormy's greatest adventures he sailed *The Courser* a long way out into the Atlantic. He wanted to catch giant tuna fish to sell in Boston.

'We'll catch lots of tuna,' Stormy told his crew.

Stormy stopped *The Courser* and dropped the ship's anchor into the water to stop *The Courser* moving. Then Stormy and his crew started to catch fish.

'Look at all of those fish!' cried the men. 'We'll catch a mountain of fish today!'

The other men used fishing rods to catch the big fish. But Stormy just caught them with his hands!

Soon, there was a giant pile of tuna on *The Courser*. Stormy even caught some sharks.

Suddenly, something from deep in the sea pulled on the anchor chain. It was something big. It almost pulled the ship under the water!

Stormy and his crew tried to pull the anchor up. They couldn't do it. The anchor didn't move!

'I'll get the anchor', said Stormy, and he dived into the water.

Stormy swam down to the bottom of the ocean. A giant octopus was holding the anchor with its eight arms! It looked like a sea monster, but Stormy wasn't scared.

Stormy started to fight with the octopus. He pulled its arms off the anchor. The octopus tried to grab Stormy, but Stormy tied up the monster's arms.

Soon Stormy had got the anchor, and he brought it back to the ship.

Back on the ship, Stormy told his crew about the octopus.

'It was the biggest sea monster I have ever seen!' he said. 'But it won't bother us again.'

The crew all cheered. Then, they sailed off to have another adventure.

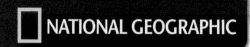
# Facts About Sea Animals

The sea is filled with amazing creatures—
some huge, some ugly and some scary.

### Megamouth Shark

The megamouth shark is about 4 to 5
metres (13 to 16 feet) long and has a
giant mouth. To eat, it swims around
with its mouth open and lets tiny sea
animals float in.

## Oarfish

The oarfish is one of the longest fish in the sea. Some oarfish are longer than 15 metres (about 50 feet) and weigh almost 272 kilograms (600 pounds). People on ships a long time ago thought oarfish were real sea monsters.

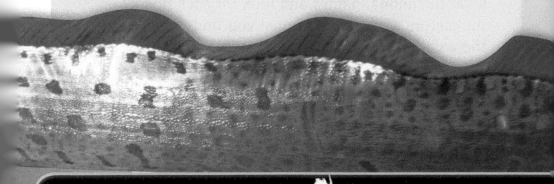

## Anglerfish

The anglerfish is only about 1 metre (3 feet) long, but its big mouth and huge teeth make it look like a monster. Anglerfish are able to make part of their bodies light up. Other fish see the light and swim to it. Then the anglerfish eats them!

## Giant Isopod

This sea creature looks like a huge underwater insect. The giant isopod lives thousands of metres down at the bottom of the sea. It can grow to be 61 centimetres (24 inches) long and weigh almost 2 kilograms (4 pounds).

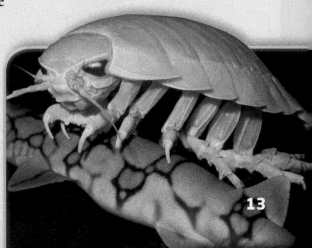

# Fun with Sea Animals

Read the animal names and look for each one in the picture. Circle each animal you find. Then list the animals in the chart from biggest to smallest.

| fish | octopus | turtle | shark | whale |
|------|---------|--------|-------|-------|

**Biggest**

_whale_

_____

_____

_____

_____

**Smallest**

**Write a word from page 14 that completes each sentence.**

1. A _____fish_____ lives in the water.

2. A _____ has a hard shell on its back.

3. An _____ has eight arms.

4. A _____ has big teeth.

5. A _____ is the biggest animal in the sea.

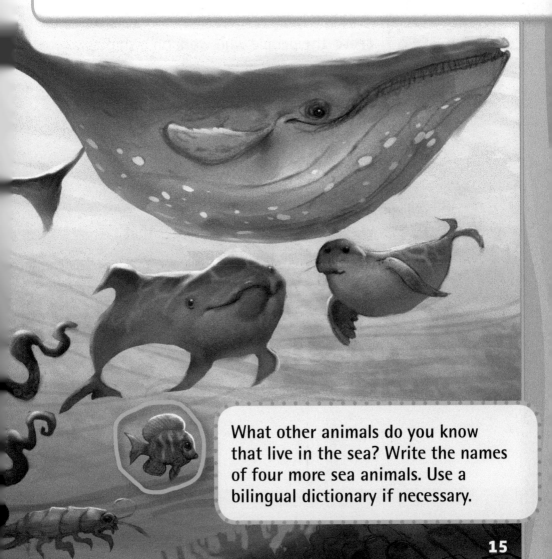

What other animals do you know that live in the sea? Write the names of four more sea animals. Use a bilingual dictionary if necessary.

# Glossary

anchor

chain

**adventures**  exciting times

**anchor**  a heavy metal object that stops ships from moving

**captain**  the person in charge of a ship

**chain**  a line made up of rings that are connected to each other

**crew**  the people who work on a ship

**giant**  very big

**monster**  a scary creature that is not real

**sail**  travel across the ocean

**tuna**  a type of large fish

**wave**  a long section of water that moves across the ocean

wave